FOREWORD

Without question, marriage is under attack like never before. It is a sad testimony to our culture that people are actually changing the vows in their wedding ceremony, substituting "as long as we both shall live," to "for as long as our love shall last," or "until our time is over." They have doomed it before ever beginning! Many people will spend more time thinking about what they'll wear for a one-hour ceremony than what they will do to build a strong marriage that should last the rest of their lives on earth. They spend more time building a house than a home.

"In spite of recent Census data, showing that fewer Americans are getting married with each passing decade, more than nine out of ten Americans eventually get married."[1] These are among the findings from a study by the Barna Research Group of Ventura, California. Unfortunately, the U.S. Census Bureau tells us over one-third of those marriages will end in divorce.

We hear the phrase, "they have a marriage made in heaven." This statement implies that some marriages are destined to be good. And if we take the flip side of that, some marriages are destined to be bad. It is as though marriage has a life all its own. Having a happy and strong marriage is no accident; it is the result of effort on the part of the partners involved.

Bill Stonebraker has attacked this important topic head-on in this new book. Bill is a good friend of mine and clearly knows what he is talking about. He and his wife Danita have been married for over forty years and have effectively pastored and counseled couples of all ages in having blessed and strong marriages.

Bill has given you a firm foundation upon which to build long and lasting relationships, whether you are considering marriage or are already married. He has identified specific traits that we can all learn from, found in the pages of the often-neglected but powerful book of Ruth. If you are single, these traits are things you should look for in potential mates. If you are already married, they are attributes to build up within yourself to be a better husband or wife.

This book is going to help you to *find* and *be* the right person in a strong and successful Christian marriage. I happily recommend it to you.

—Greg Laurie,
Pastor and Evangelist

What Calvary Pastors are saying about
The Right Choice by Bill Stonebraker

I welcome Pastor Bill Stonebraker's clarion call to singles, engaged couples, and married couples to come back to the timeless truths found in the book of Ruth regarding God's will for our marriages. Culturally current and richly relevant, Bill has taught these truths from the pulpit, counseled many with their wisdom, and lived them out in his forty years of marriage to Danita. As a pastor, husband, and father, I am grateful for his skillful handling of the Word of God on this subject."

Bob Coy, pastor of Calvary Chapel Fort Lauderdale, Florida, and author of *Devotionary*

In today's world, with the continuing AIDS epidemic and divorce at its highest, Pastor Bill Stonebraker has written *The Right Choice: Discerning God's Will in Choosing a Mate* for such a time as this. Being single and looking for a mate can be very stressful. In this book, Bill gives great insight to singles on how to follow God's will in finding a godly mate."

Raul Ries, pastor of Calvary Chapel Golden Springs, Diamond Bar, California, and author of *Fury to Freedom*

Bill Stonebraker weaves the story of Ruth into an excellent tapestry for marriage and courtship with insight and illustrations that will keep you reading."

Gayle Erwin, director of Servant's Quarters in Cathedral City, California, and author of *The Jesus Style*

Human relationships in harmony is a subject about which the Bible speaks very clearly. Proverbs teaches: 'If a man would have friends, he must show himself to be friendly.' Bill Stonebraker is a friend's friend. Read this book with expectation and learn how to follow God's voice and have wonderful relationships. This is a must read!"

Mike MacIntosh, pastor of Horizon Christian Fellowship in San Diego, California, and author of *For the Love of Mike*

the RIGHT *choice*

Discerning God's Will in Choosing a Mate

BILL STONEBRAKER

CALVARY CHAPEL
PUBLISHING

The Right Choice
Discerning God's Will in Choosing a Mate

Copyright © 2007 by Bill Stonebraker

Published by Calvary Chapel Publishing (CCP),
a resource ministry of Calvary Chapel of Costa Mesa
3800 South Fairview Road
Santa Ana, CA 92704

First printing, 2007

Passages from the book of Ruth and all other Scripture, unless otherwise noted, is taken from the NEW AMERICAN STANDARD BIBLE®. Copyright © The Lockman Foundation 1960, 1962, 1963, 1968, 1971, 1972, 1973, 1975, 1977, 1995. Used by permission. All rights reserved.

Scripture quotations marked (TLB) are taken from The Living Bible, copyright © 1971. Used by permission of Tyndale House Publishers, Inc., Wheaton, Illinois 60189. All rights reserved.

Cover layout and design by David Riley Associates, Costa Mesa, CA
Inside page layout by Bob Bubnis at BookSetters

ISBN 10: 1-59751-023-8
ISBN 13: 978-1-59751-023-3

Printed in the United States of America.

DEDICATION

This book is dedicated to all those who will one day be married and who desire to make a wise and godly decision when choosing that mate.

ACKNOWLEDGMENTS

My wife, Danita, gets high marks when it comes to possessing the Ruth-like qualities discussed in this book. She is also a great motivator for me to develop the Boaz-like traits I would like to see in myself.

TABLE OF CONTENTS

PREFACE

Sometimes when studying the Bible, spiritual *manna* seems to drop from heaven. This happened to me as I was preparing to teach the book of Ruth — a wonderful story that illustrates our redemption so beautifully. Character traits of Ruth and Boaz seemed to jump off the pages at me. The providence of God brought these two together, but the preparation of their individual lives was an ongoing process.

Reading the book of Ruth, we see which characteristics made Ruth and Boaz attractive to each other, and in so doing, we get a good idea of what we should look for when choosing a husband or wife. Plus, we learn what the desirable traits are that need to be developed in us.

ONE

Open to Change?

There are specific and identifiable qualities in the kind of people who get married and stay married. These traits are fundamental to developing good relationships and a good marriage. For the single person looking to marry one day, there are particular attributes you possess that will be attractive to the opposite sex, and there are qualities that you will find appealing in a potential mate. For the married person, there are traits you can develop to strengthen and revitalize your relationship. These qualities, found in the book of Ruth, will ensure a strong and healthy marriage *until death do you part.*

God created the man and the woman. He also created marriage, and He knows how marriage works best. Genesis 2:18 tells us, "Then the LORD God said, 'It is not good for the man to be alone; I will make him a helper suitable [or fit] for him." He knows what will make two people "fit." He knows the character qualities that are needed in marriage partners for their compatibility and how to realize the principle in Genesis 2:24 of the *two becoming one.*

No matter what your current marital status the biblical principles in this study will be beneficial to you.

- Perhaps you will be single your entire life. In that case, embrace the godly attributes and characteristics found in Boaz and Ruth. Jesus is your life partner.

- If you are a single person who desires one day to be married, these are qualities you should look for in a mate. They are also attributes you should develop in yourself in preparation for marriage.

- If you are already married, these are character traits that are attractive to your mate and that will keep your marriage exciting, growing, and full of wonder.

Oscar

Married couples are always discovering and revealing new things about each other, no matter how long they have been married. Danita and I have been married now for over four decades, and yet just recently I learned something new about her.

We got an Oscar fish, which can grow fairly large (we are on our third fish tank). We were feeding him regular fish pellets when one day Danita came home with a container full of goldfish. I asked, "Hun, what are you going to do with those fish?" and she replied with a grin, "I'm going to feed them to Oscar (we also named the fish Oscar)." I couldn't hide my surprise. "You're going to feed the goldfish to Oscar? I never knew you had that in you!"

My wife is very sympathetic and tenderhearted; she pampers and spoils every pet she has ever had. Yet with absolute glee she put a goldfish into the tank, and we watched as Oscar went nose-to-nose with it. Next thing we know, all we could see was the tail of the goldfish protruding from Oscar's mouth. He swallowed it whole in one gulp. Then with delight Danita put another goldfish into the tank.

I've come to understand that Oscar fish eat smaller varieties, called "feeder fish," but I kid Danita about this because I didn't think she had it in her. I thought she was such a softy, and that the goldfishes would have their own little bowl side-by-side with Oscar. I never imagined they'd be Oscar's dinner—fed to him by the hand of my sweet wife!

Never think that you have got your mate all figured out or that there is nothing new to discover about them because they just might do something that will totally surprise you.

A woman named Charlene related this story:

George and I were engaged in a lively conversation when he stopped talking a moment and retrieved his white, no-frills hanky out of his back pocket. Unfolding it, he vigorously blew his nose. I continued to talk without skipping a beat. After several good snorts, he folded the hanky right on the creases again and again, until it was returned to its perfect square. He put it in his right hand and slid it down into his back pocket.

When he looked up at me, I had become mute. My mouth was agape. I couldn't believe what I was seeing, and it showed on my face. "Is something wrong?" he asked.

"Do you always fold your hanky like that after you blow your nose?"

"Yes," he said. "Is that a problem?"

"Maybe," I answered.

"Why?"

"After 20 years of married life," I told him, "I had no idea you folded your hanky back up like that after blowing your nose."

"So?" he asked.

"So? So, I'm sorry to tell you that when I am doing the laundry and find the hanky so neatly folded in your back pocket, I assume it hasn't been used and I simply put it back in the drawer without washing it!"

Now it was George's turn to stare with his mouth wide open. But after a couple beats passed, he remarked, "No wonder I always have so much trouble getting my glasses clean . . ."

Some of the new discoveries we make about our mates we like, and others we don't. A cartoon pictures a woman sitting in a marriage counselor's office. The caption reads: "When I first got married, I was looking for the ideal; then it turned into an ordeal; now I'm looking for a new deal." Another man, speaking about his marriage, said, "It's been like a three-ring circus: first the engagement ring, then the wedding ring, now the *suffer*-ring."

When you get married and you discover those things about your mate that rub you the wrong way, how do you react? Is it possible to "shockproof" your marriage, or at least minimize the surprise?

One of the best ways to prepare yourself for marriage is to develop those personal attributes that are attractive in a mate. When choosing God's choice of a husband or wife, it is important to know what to look for in the person with whom you plan to spend the rest of your life. And they need to see comparable qualities in you.

The book of Ruth is a treasure-trove of knowledge that focuses on the attributes of a woman worth marrying. It reveals the godly traits in the woman Ruth that are attractive to a man. The book also highlights characteristics of a man worth marrying. It describes the godly qualities of the man Boaz that are attractive to a woman. The four chapters in Ruth are a recipe for identifying the kind of person whose character qualities have been developed before marriage, so that when marriage comes there will be compatibility and companionability.

TEST YOURSELF

Here in chapter one we have looked at the first of several specific and identifiable qualities in the kind of people who get married and stay married: openness to change, or flexibility.

1. For those of you who are married:

   a. What is one *positive* thing you discovered about your mate only after you married them?

   b. What is one thing about yourself that you think surprised your mate after the wedding vows?

   c. What are some areas you have yielded in over the course of your marriage?

   d. What are some areas in which you see the need for more flexibility in your life?

2. For those of you who are single:

    a. What types of things challenge your flexibility in relationships? Over what types of things do you struggle with giving up control?

    b. Is there anything over which you should be uncompromising?

    c. Can you think of an example in any relationship you have had where you "gave up your rights" for the sake of unity?

    Was it a good decision?

    d. What is the biggest change you have ever had to make in your life, and how did you handle it?

TWO

Purity in an Impure World

The book of Ruth was written during the age of the judges in Israel. The phrase that became a mantra for those turbulent times was "Every man did what was right in his own eyes" (Judges 17:6). It was a time of social upheaval, moral chaos, and spiritual anarchy. The people of God were in rebellion against Him. The social norm among the Jews was loose living, political turmoil, and religious debauchery.

However, within this framework of moral mayhem and spiritual apostasy, Ruth and Boaz remained faithful to God. They stayed pure morally when it was cool to sleep around. They remained true to God when it was politically correct to have a tolerant, inclusive, and liberal belief system.

An article in *USA TODAY* talked about changes in television. It noted that a generation ago we did not see on TV what we see now. Today television is constantly pushing the limits, the article stated. There are sexually perverted people who come up with shows that promote promiscuity, celebrate homosexuality, and are attempting to recreate the cultural norm. This is in contrast to shows aired a generation ago in which there was a traditional family, with both father and mother, and some sense of morality.

Today everything has changed. According to media moguls, writers, producers, and others who influence what is shown at the movies, on television, and in print, the accepted lifestyle is to be sexually active. Sleeping around is a normal, natural way to live, and if you are sexually pure and remain a virgin until marriage, there is something wrong with you.

The article, entitled "Study Suggests Teen Sex Linked to Depression, Suicide Tries" went on to say:

> A controversial new study links teen sexual intercourse with depression and suicide attempts. The findings are particularly true for young girls, says the Heritage Foundation, a conservative think tank that sponsored the research. About 25% of sexually active girls say they are depressed all, most or a lot of the time; 8% of girls who are not sexually active say they feel the same . . . The study findings send a clear message about unhappy teens that differs from one portrayed in the popular culture, that "all forms of non-marital sexual activity are wonderful and glorious, particularly the younger (teen) the better."

Note: Over three times as many girls (300% more) who engage in sexual activity before marriage are struggling with depression, as compared to those girls who are not sexually active.

> "The Heritage study goes on to find: About 14% of girls who have had intercourse have attempted suicide; 5% of sexually inactive girls have. About 6% of sexually active boys have tried suicide; fewer than 1% of sexually inactive boys have."[2]

Note: Almost three times as many sexually active girls try to commit suicide, compared to those who are not sexually active. And a whopping six times as many boys (600% more) who are sexually active attempt suicide, as compared to those who are not sexually active!

This should be a wake-up call to our young people. The culture of promiscuity, driven by television, movies, magazines, and music, is seeking to redefine our social norms. But they've got it all wrong . . . dead wrong.

The same social changes and challenges taking place in our day were also happening during the time of the book of Ruth. Boaz and Ruth met those challenges and steadfastly followed the Lord. It is important for us to learn how to develop those same biblical attributes. They are traits that are attractive in a mate.

The book of Ruth will make clear what you should look for in the person you will eventually marry and what they should be looking for in you. Also, if you are already married, these are qualities you don't want to let slip away once the vows are spoken and the ring is on the finger. More than ever you want to stir up, rekindle, perfect, and progress in them so that as the years go by marital life will get better and better. In fact, speaking from my own experience, it doesn't just get better but *incredibly* better — "abundantly above all you can ask or think."

TEST YOURSELF

It has become acceptable and even normal in our culture to sleep around, to have sex with your boyfriend or girlfriend. Those who are determined to stay pure and chaste until marriage are looked down upon, scoffed at, and made to feel that they are abnormal. And yet statistics show that those who are promiscuous are having more serious emotional and relational problems.

1. How do you think the media influences what we think about: Masculinity? Femininity? Modern male/female relationships?

2. Is biblical morality unrealistic? Why or why not?

3. What are some specific changes you can make in your life to safeguard your own purity in this impure world?

4. What are some practical things you can do to strengthen yourself against the temptations of sexual sin?

THREE

But God Has a Plan

We now begin the incredible journey to discover the awesome attributes of our two main characters: Ruth and Boaz. So we begin reading in the book of Ruth, chapter 1:

> Now it came about in the days when the judges governed, that there was a famine in the land. And a certain man of Bethlehem in Judah went to sojourn in the land of Moab with his wife and his two sons. And the name of the man was Elimelech, and the name of his wife, Naomi; and the names of his two sons were Mahlon and Chilion, Ephrathites of Bethlehem in Judah. Now they entered the land of Moab and remained there. (1:1–2)

Literally the names *Mahlon* and *Chilion* meant "sickly" and "piney." Back in those days, parents named their children after some circumstance surrounding the birth. For example, Isaac's wife, Rebekah, had a difficult pregnancy with her twins, and the Lord spoke to her, saying: "Two nations are in your womb; and two peoples shall be separated from your body" (Genesis 25:23). When the boys were born, the first came out covered with hair, so he was named *Esau* which means "hairy." Next came *Jacob*, which means "heelcatcher" — so named because he was holding on to his brother's heel.

So we can assume that Mahlon and Chilion were not the picture of health when they were born. They likely were somewhat anemic-looking, so they were named *Sickly* and *Piney*.

Elimelech and his family were from Bethlehem. The name *Bethlehem* means "place of bread" or "house of bread." However, they were now in a place of famine. Why? God was judging His people for their rebellion and apostasy. So Elimelech decided to move to another location where they might find sustenance. He led his family to Moab — a pagan land.

> Then Elimelech, Naomi's husband, died; and she was left and her two sons. And they took for themselves Moabite women as wives; the name of the one was Orpah and the name of the other Ruth. And they lived there about ten years. Then both Mahlon and Chilion also died; and the woman was bereft of her two sons and her husband. (1:3–5)

Sometime after the family moved to Moab, Elimelech died. Naomi was left with her two sons, and sought out two Moabite women that would be willing to marry *Sickly* and *Piney*. A short while later the two sons died — not surprising when you take into account that they were frail from birth. So Naomi endured not only the loss of her husband, but her two children as well.

Obviously, this was a very difficult time for Naomi. She went to a new land because of God's judgment upon Bethlehem, and when she got there her husband and two sons died. She was going through a terrible trial. Perhaps Elimelech was self-directed, not God-directed, when he took his family to Moab; and now Naomi was left to pick up the pieces. Fortunately, God's sovereignty can override our bad decisions.

> Then she [Naomi] arose with her daughters-in-law that she might return from the country of Moab, for she had heard

in the land of Moab that the LORD had visited His people by giving them food. So she departed from the place where she was, and her two daughters-in-law with her; and they went on the way to return to the land of Judah. (1:6–7)

Naomi's Hard Decision

Naomi had no one in the world now. She relied upon her two daughters-in-law for comfort and strength in this very difficult time. Maybe she suffered in silence, but the pain on her face was unmistakable. She contemplated going back to her own land, Bethlehem; and as she considered the hardship her two Moabite daughters-in-law would face there, she told them: "Why don't you go back to your mothers' houses. You are young women; you can still marry again within your own culture."

> And Naomi said to her two daughters-in-law, "Go, return each of you to her mother's house. May the LORD deal kindly with you as you have dealt with the dead and with me. May the LORD grant that you may find rest, each in the house of her husband." Then she kissed them, and they lifted up their voices and wept. And they said to her, "No, but we will surely return with you to your people." But Naomi said, "Return, my daughters. Why should you go with me? Have I yet sons in my womb, that they may be your husbands? Return, my daughters! Go, for I am too old to have a husband. If I said I have hope, if I should even have a husband tonight and also bear sons, would you wait until they were grown? Would you refrain yourselves from marrying? No, my daughters; for it is harder for me than for you, for the hand of the LORD has gone forth against me." (1:8–13)

Naomi was saying, "It will be a hardship if you go with me, because Jewish custom would require you to marry within the family and I have no more children for you to wed. Don't wait around; even if I could bear more sons, it is unreasonable to think you would wait until they were old enough to marry. Go back home and find new husbands in your own land."

God was working in Naomi's life even though she was in despair. She did not see the hand of God at this time because of all the hurt and pain.

That is often the case when you settle into a place of discouragement. When you are overcome with despair, it is difficult to see God working. A penny can block out the sun if you put it right in front of your eye; in the same way, your problems can block out God. Yet the truth is, the sun and the Son are far greater than any penny or problem. It's all a matter of perspective.

During times of trial, we can easily become pessimistic and unbelieving. We are convinced that our situation will never change, that things will never turn around for us. We can literally worry ourselves sick when we stop trusting God. It's been said, "Worry is like a rocking chair: it gives us something to do, but it doesn't get us anywhere!"

When despair sets in, like it did with Naomi, you can begin to think, "Everything is going against me, nothing is going for me," and that your desperate situation will never change. But you are wrong. If you are a child of God and are trusting in Him, you may be going through the deepest and darkest trial of your life, things may appear completely hopeless, *but God has a plan!*

TEST YOURSELF

Everyone goes through stages in their Christian lives in which they feel down and out, or are in a place of discouragement or despair. It is not wrong to have these down times. What matters is how you deal with them.

These difficult times can often occur right when we have important decisions to make. Seeking the counsel of the Lord, in the Word, in prayer, through church leaders or other mature believers, can reassure us that *God has a plan* for our lives.

1. Tell about a difficult decision you have had to make in your life. How did you approach it?

2. What do you do when you get discouraged?

3. What *should* you do when you get discouraged?

4. Can a person safeguard his or herself against disappointment?

   If so, how; if not, why not?

FOUR

Ruth Is Devoted

God had a plan for Naomi, but there was also a test for Orpah and Ruth:

> And then they lifted up their voices and wept again; and Orpah kissed her mother-in-law, but Ruth clung to her. (1:14)

Considering Naomi's state of mind at this time, we discover a big difference between the two daughters-in-law, revealed by the decision each made. Orpah kissed Naomi and said good-bye, while Ruth clung to her in devotion and loyalty.

> Then she said [to Ruth], "Behold, your sister-in-law has gone back to her people and to her gods; return after your sister-in-law." But Ruth said, "Do not urge me to leave you or to turn back from following after you; for where you go, I will go; and where you lodge, I will lodge. Your people shall be my people, and your God, my God. Where you die, I will die, and there I will be buried. Thus may the LORD do to me, and worse, if anything but death parts you and me." When she saw that she was determined to go with her, she said no more to her. (1:15–18)

Ruth does not display a *me-first attitude* but one of self-less **devotion**. It is an attribute that a man finds very attractive in a woman.

Danita and I were childhood sweethearts—and I do mean *childhood*—she was 13 and I was 17 when we first met. One of the things that attracted me to her was her selfless devotion. Ruth's devotion was to her mother-in-law, but this trait can be directed in many ways. In Danita's case, her pets were the objects of her devotion. She had dogs, turtles, and rabbits, and I saw that she treated her animals with tender, loving care. I certainly did not have the patience to nurse a baby hamster back to health with a baby-doll's bottle, but she did. (*Oscar* taught me that goldfish apparently are a different case.)

It is this quality of being "others centered," of being loyal and having empathy for another person or even a pet, that is very attractive. It is a nurturing quality within a woman that starts at an early age and continues as she grows and matures.

When a man sees these domestic home-fires kindled and burning in a woman, it is very attractive to him. He appreciates the fact that her focus is outside of herself. She is not constantly in front of the mirror primping and pampering herself; there is more to her than simply being self-absorbed.

Does TV Define Who We Are?

I don't understand the appeal of many of the new "reality" television shows. What is the fascination with following around pseudo-celebrities twenty-four hours a day? We have seen the most bizarre behavior from people like Anna Nicole Smith, Bobby Brown, Paris Hilton, and others, *ad nauseam*. Are these the people we want to hold up as role models: men and women we want to emulate, or are they simply quirky and peculiar? It's like looking at the Elephant man, John Merrick: we know we shouldn't stare but we can't help ourselves.

What is so fascinating about the Osbourne family? Are they our generation's *Ozzie and Harriet*? What quality in Ozzy Osbourne do we want to pattern our lives after: Obscenities?

Our culture and attitudes are drifting downward quickly, moving away from what we see here in Ruth, with her selfless devotion. The man may be called of God to be the head of the family, but the woman is the *heart*. Ruth had a lot of heart. She had selfless devotion.

> So they both went until they came to Bethlehem. And it came about when they had come to Bethlehem, that all the city was stirred because of them; and the women said, "Is this Naomi?" And she said to them, "Do not call me Naomi; call me Mara, for the Almighty has dealt very bitterly with me. I went out full, but the LORD has brought me back empty. Why do you call me Naomi, since the LORD has witnessed against me and the Almighty has afflicted me?" (1:19–21)

The name *Naomi* means "pleasant." Formerly Naomi had a pleasant disposition and a happy nature, but that has changed and she no longer wants to be called by that name. "That is not me anymore," she is saying. "Call me Mara"—meaning *bitter*—"because bitterness now defines who I am."

Perhaps Naomi wore her sorrow visibly: grief lines may have creased her brow, despair deadened her eyes, and a frown was permanently fixed on her face. What Naomi was feeling would not last long, however. God had a future and a hope in store for her. God was working a work that would soon cause her heart to sing and her face to shine with the joy of the Lord. She was about to see the hand of God ruling over her bitter circumstances.

If God could work in Naomi's life, He can work in yours. Do not allow difficulties and hardships to define who you are, or to dictate your feelings or your faith. Be encouraged to follow the Lord, even when things are not going your way, when situations are not turning out the way you expected. Remember Jeremiah 29:11: "For I know the plans that I have for you," declares the LORD, "plans for welfare and not for calamity to give you a future and a hope." God has a future and a hope for you. Stay the course; run the race; be faithful to His path and He will do abundantly above all you could ask or think. The Lord will perform the spectacular; He will astonish and amaze you.

TEST YOURSELF

We talked about the "me first" mentality of our culture; people today are looking out for number one. Surely some of us would not blame Orpah and Ruth for going back to their own families and culture in order to marry again and have families of their own.

Ruth does something that to some might look like a mistake in the beginning. As the story unfolds, however, we discover God's hand upon her life and His divine providence in putting her in the right place at the right time. It all begins with selfless devotion.

1. What does loyalty *look like*?

    a. What does a loyal person do?

    b. What do they not do?

2. In what way does selfless devotion to a person require faith in God?

3. Can you think of a time when someone displayed loyalty to you?

How did it make you feel?

4. When she chose to remain with Naomi, Ruth was entrusting her future to Naomi's God. When two people enter into a marital relationship, are they entrusting their future to each other or to God? Explain your answer.

FIVE

Ruth Is Productive

God is about to do something wonderful—not only in the disheartened Naomi, who lost her husband, her two sons, and her optimism—but also in Ruth, whose selfless devotion is about to be rewarded.

> So Naomi returned, and with her Ruth the Moabitess, her daughter-in-law, who returned from the land of Moab. And they came to Bethlehem at the beginning of barley harvest. Now Naomi had a kinsman of her husband, a man of great wealth, of the family of Elimelech; whose name was Boaz. And Ruth the Moabitess said to Naomi, "Please let me go to the field and glean ears of grain after one in whose sight I may find favor." And she said to her, "Go, my daughter." (1:22–2:2)

It was extremely dangerous back then for an attractive foreigner to glean in an unfamiliar field. There were unprincipled men who could stalk a woman, take advantage of her, and even rape her if they thought they could get away with it. Yet where sin abounds, grace does much more abound (Romans 5:20). In this case, God's hand was on Ruth, protecting her and keeping her safe from any predators.

Naomi and Ruth were indigent at this point; they had nothing. As Naomi put it: "I went out full, but the LORD has brought me

37

back empty" (1:21). The women were destitute, penniless. There was no government-subsidized welfare system in Bethlehem; there was no one to support them. What were their options? They could sit around and starve, they could beg for food, or they could go and glean in someone's field.

The closest thing to a "welfare system" in ancient Israel, established by Moses in the Law, was an opportunity for the poor and needy to go into someone's field and pick up what was dropped or missed by the harvesters. It was difficult work, requiring long hours, and Naomi had reached an age where she was too old and feeble to handle it. But Ruth eagerly volunteered.

Here we see another characteristic in Ruth that sets her apart from other women: she was **productive**. Ruth is willing to work and work hard. This is the second attribute that makes a woman attractive and desirable to a man for a marriage partner.

The Bible speaks of the industrious woman in Proverbs 31: "She looks for wool and flax, and works with her hands in delight. She is like merchant ships; she brings her food from afar. She rises also while it is still night, and gives food to her household, and portions to her maidens. She considers a field and buys it; from her earnings she plants a vineyard. She girds herself with strength, and makes her arms strong. She senses that her gain is good; her lamp does not go out at night" (vv. 13–18). There is a special quality about a woman who is productive and hard-working, who takes it upon herself to get done what needs to be done. It is an admirable quality.

Again, I look to the example of my wife, Danita. When she was young and still living at home with her family, one of her household chores was doing the laundry. Her parents did not have a washer and dryer, so she had to take the clothes to the laundromat. Being the boyfriend, I of course would help her. There would be baskets and baskets full of laundry, which we would pile into the back of my station wagon. There at the laundromat, we would load up five or six machines with all the dirty clothes.

Danita knew how to sort the whites from the colors, to put the delicates in their own machine, and so on. When they were finished washing and drying, she would fold everything just right: dress shirts, t-shirts, jeans, linens, and towels. She was incredibly fast. I would help, but it was like the Tortoise and the Hare: for every one item I folded, she folded five or six. I still remember those times and I still admire that in her. She was very industrious. And she hasn't changed over the years; in fact, she is more productive today than ever.

Slugs Are Not Attractive

A man or woman who is non-productive will eventually grate on the other person's nerves. Slugs are not very attractive. A woman who regularly uses her gifts and talents, hobbies and interests, and is industrious in those things, really intrigues a man. A man likes a woman who is independent, self-sufficient, and capable; it's very appealing to him.

Genesis 24 tells the story of Abraham sending his servant Eleazar to find a wife for his son, Isaac. He sent him to relatives in Mesopotamia. When Eleazar came to the city of Nahor, he stopped by a well at evening time, and when the women came out to draw water he prayed: "O LORD, the God of my master Abraham, please grant me success today, and show lovingkindness to my master Abraham. Behold, I am standing by the spring, and the daughters of the men of the city are coming out to draw water; now may it be that the girl to whom I say, 'Please let down your jar so that I may drink,' and who answers, 'Drink, and I will water your camels also';—may she be the one whom Thou hast appointed for Thy servant Isaac; and by this I shall know that Thou hast shown lovingkindness to my master" (Genesis 24:12–14).

That was an interesting "fleece" laid out before the Lord (see Judges 6 for Gideon's use of a "fleece" to determine God's will). Eleazar realized there were qualities in an productive woman that would go a long way when seeking God's choice for a mate.

> "Before he had finished speaking, that behold, Rebekah who was born to Bethuel the son of Milcah, the wife of Abraham's brother Nahor, came out with her jar on her shoulder. And the girl was very beautiful, a virgin, and no man had had relations with her; and she went down to the spring and filled her jar, and came up. Then the servant ran to meet her, and said, 'Please let me drink a little water from your jar.' And she said, 'Drink, my lord'; and she quickly lowered her jar to her hand, and gave him a drink. Now when she had finished giving him a drink, she said, 'I will draw also for your camels until they have finished drinking'" (Genesis 24:15–19).

Drawing water for the camels was not a simple task. Eleazar had ten camels, each of which easily could drink twenty gallons of water. Rebekah didn't consider how hard the task would be; she simply wanted to meet the need. That might have been two hundred gallons of water, which spoke volumes about her character.

TEST YOURSELF

A woman who shows fortitude in whatever she does will be successful whether she is married or not. There is something about this type of woman that finds her rising to the top of whatever she does.

The problem comes when a man is threatened by her ability. Some men want a workhorse kind of woman when it comes to cleaning, cooking, and generally taking care of him. However, a wife is not an indentured servant and should never be treated that way.

1. Genesis 2:15 tells us: "Then the LORD God took the man and put him into the garden of Eden to cultivate it and keep it."

   Can you think of any reasons why God would have men and women work, even in Paradise?

2. How do you feel when you accomplish something meaningful or difficult?

3. Who benefits when a person works hard? Explain your answer.

4. In many modern marriages, both husband and wife are bread-winners.

    a. What are some of the pitfalls to avoid when both have obligations outside and inside of the home?

    b. How can that affect the roles of husbands and wives?

5. Today's society often sees stay-at-home wives and moms as unsuccessful.

Do you think a career wife is more productive than a stay-at-home-wife?

Explain your answer.

SIX

Boaz Is Respectful

We pick up the story in chapter 2, where Ruth is asking permission of Naomi to glean in the field. Harvest time had come and almost gone, and without gleaning the women would otherwise go hungry.

> So she departed and went and gleaned in the field after the reapers; and she happened to come to the portion of the field belonging to Boaz, who was of the family of Elimelech. (2:3)

Remember Elimelech? He was Naomi's husband. Boaz was from the family tree of Elimelech and therefore a close relative who could marry Ruth!

> Now behold, Boaz came from Bethlehem and said to the reapers, "May the LORD be with you" And they said to him, "May the LORD bless you." (2:4)

Here we see in Boaz the first of several attributes that are very attractive in a man: he is **respectful**. He respects his workers, and in turn, he is respected by them.

Respect is a quality worth cultivating. You can start practicing it today. Whether you are a boss or a regular employee, show esteem and respect for others. It should be a mutual, two-way street. If you are a person who treasures friendships, esteems family members, and shows basic respect for others, you are like Boaz. Respect is not something you do for show, but rather it is ingrained in your character. It is a quality a woman finds very desirable in a man. In fact, Proverbs 22:1 teaches that: "A good name is to be more desired than great riches, favor is better than silver and gold."

We can ruin our reputation by doing foolish things, by treating people poorly, as though they were less than ourselves. We don't realize how it alienates those people looking on as they observe us lording it over others. However, when we display respect for others, when we esteem and value people, we find it is a very attractive quality to a potential spouse, as the case was with Boaz.

Boaz Is Attentive

> Then Boaz said to his servant who was in charge of the reapers, "Whose young woman is this?" And the servant in charge of the reapers answered and said, "She is the young Moabite woman who returned with Naomi from the land of Moab. And she said, 'Please let me glean and gather after the reapers among the sheaves.' Thus she came and has remained from the morning until now; she has been sitting in the house for a little while." (2:5–7)

What is appealing here is that Boaz is **attentive** to Ruth. He notices her, he inquires about her, and he considers her. It is very attractive to a woman when a man pays attention to her—in a good way, that is.

There were scoundrels reaping in the fields who were on the make. They would pay attention to women in an immoral way, putting them into compromising situations in order to get what they wanted from them. This was not true of Boaz, however. He took an interest in Ruth and paid attention to her for who she *was*, and not for what he could *take* from her.

Boaz Is Kind

> Then Boaz said to Ruth, "Listen carefully, my daughter. Do not go to glean in another field; furthermore, do not go on from this one, but stay here with my maids. Let your eyes be on the field which they reap, and go after them. Indeed, I have commanded the servants not to touch you. When you are thirsty, go to the water jars and drink from what the servants draw." (2:8–9)

Boaz is shown to be **kind.** Typically when a woman identifies the qualities she feels would be absolutely necessary in the man she would marry, kindness is near the top of the list. It is very important to a woman that a man is kind to her. Proverbs 19:22 says, "What is desirable in a man is his kindness."

Boaz provides for Ruth; he tells her where to get water to drink. He also protects her by instructing his servants not to touch her. He looks out for Ruth, shielding and safeguarding her from any harm. A man who is kind, without any ulterior motives, causes a woman to feel secure in his presence.

TEST YOURSELF

In rapid succession, we have seen three traits in Boaz that seem so natural, we might overlook them when simply reading through the story: respect, attentiveness, and kindness. As we take a closer look, we begin to get a better portrait of this man, and we find some important questions to ask ourselves.

1. Romans 12:10 tells us to "outdo one another in showing honor" (TLB).

   Many people believe that respect is earned. Is that what the Bible teaches? Explain.

2. Respect for a person can grow beyond just the basics that we would show to anyone.

   a. What cultivates greater respect in you for someone?

   b. What are some practical ways a person can show respect for their mate?

c. What are some things to avoid because they demonstrate disrespect?

3. Philippians 2:3 says "each of you regard one another as more important than himself."

a. What does attentiveness to others say about *us*?

b. How can you develop a greater attentiveness to others without being phony?

4. Kindness is defined in part as "the capability of being sympathetic and compassionate." How can attentiveness toward someone increase our *kindness* toward them?

5. Kindness is also an action. What moves you from merely being sympathetic toward someone to actually *doing* something to help?

SEVEN

Ruth Is Innocent

Notice how Ruth responds to the kindness shown to her by Boaz.

> Then she fell on her face, bowing to the ground and said
> to him, "Why have I found favor in your sight that you
> should take notice of me, since I am a foreigner?" (2:10)

I have used the term **innocent** for this attribute in Ruth in that it carries the idea of being unspoiled. She is a woman in whom there is no guile; she is unpretentious and inexperienced in the coarser things of life. This is an almost childlike quality. She thinks less of herself than what others think of her. What a beautiful attribute!

In this, Ruth is much like Mary, the mother of Jesus. Mary also had this wide-eyed characteristic. She was truly surprised that the Lord would consider her special in His sight. After the angel Gabriel came and told her that she was going to have a Child, she said: "My soul exalts the Lord, and my spirit has rejoiced in God my Savior. For He has had regard for the humble state of His bondslave; for behold, from this time on all generations will count me blessed" (Luke 1:46–48). She was astonished that she was favored in God's eyes. Like Ruth, she had that wide-eyed innocence, and it is a precious quality in a woman.

Boaz Is Appreciative

Boaz now responds to Ruth's wide-eyed innocence.

> And Boaz answered and said to her, "All that you have done for your mother-in-law after the death of your husband has been fully reported to me, and how you have left your father and your mother and the land of your birth, and have come to a people that you did not previously know. May the LORD reward your work, and your wages be full from the LORD, the God of Israel, under whose wings you have come to seek refuge." (2:11–12)

Boaz is **appreciative** of Ruth. It is endearing to a woman when she feels appreciated. Boaz is investigative; he asks questions about her. He is insightful, and then he expresses his appreciation for Ruth. It is a wonderful thing when a man values a woman for who she is as a person. This is a great quality in a man.

Boaz was able to speak about Ruth's hidden qualities because he took the time to find out about them. His was not just a physical attraction: "Wow, what a foxy chick!" If that had been the case, Ruth probably would have replied something like, "Oh, yeah? Forget you, buddy. You've got the wrong girl." But Boaz appreciated her inner beauty. He saw those hidden qualities necessary for longevity in a relationship because he investigated the kind of woman Ruth was when she was outside the gaze and scrutiny of others. And he complimented her on those qualities. He noticed her sacrificial love for her mother-in-law and all that she did for Naomi after her husband Elimelech and their two sons died. Boaz saw how Ruth committed herself to caring for Naomi, and he praised and blessed her for her godly behavior.

Ruth Is Thankful

We see another quality in Ruth in verse 13:

Then she said, "I have found favor in your sight, my lord, for you have comforted me and indeed have spoken kindly to your maidservant, though I am not like one of your maidservants." (2:13)

Ruth is **thankful** to Boaz. She confesses that he has been a comfort to her and that he has given her strength. She is grateful for such undeserved favor.

When a man does a good deed for a woman, or he compliments her, it may or may not bother him if she responds in kind. He might think he's just one of many who notice her. What a man definitely does appreciate, however, is when a woman is thankful for what he does for her. Appreciation and thankfulness are attractive to him.

Ruth Is Humble

The kindness Boaz showed toward Ruth brought out in her another desirable trait: that of being **humble,** or what we might term "self-deprecating." Ruth says, "I am not like one of your maidservants." She saw herself as less than other women, lowly and humble; she did not flaunt her beauty or generous deeds. She did not even see herself on par with Boaz's maidservants. She was genuinely humble, seeing herself as less than others esteemed her.

It is attractive to a man when a woman is modest, unaware of her hidden and obvious beauty. She esteems others more highly than herself. The effect it has on a man is that it makes him want to build her up, to let her know how valuable she is to him. Like a rosebud opens its petals into full bloom when exposed to the sun, so a woman who is praised and esteemed by her suitor will blossom and become even more beautiful.

Paul said in Romans 12:3: "For through the grace given to me I say to every man among you not to think more highly of himself than he ought to think; but to think so as to have sound judgment." Ruth had an unspoiled quality about her; she didn't think more highly of herself than she ought. She did not see herself as worthy of this special attention.

Typically the people who deserve a lot of appreciation don't see themselves in that way. However, God, in His providence, often brings someone into their lives who expresses the kind of praise that is fitting for them, as we see here in the case of Boaz and Ruth.

TEST YOURSELF

We have studied a progression of traits in Ruth and Boaz. She is innocent, she is thankful, and she is humble. He is appreciative.

1. How do humility, thankfulness, and appreciation go hand-in-hand?

   What is a common theme?

2. What is the difference between true humility and a poor self-image?

3. What are some practical ways you can express appreciation for someone?

4. When *your* thoughtful deeds are not met with appreciation, how can you stay motivated to continue them anyway?

5. What are some things we can do to cultivate a thankful heart?

EIGHT

Boaz Is Considerate

> And at mealtime Boaz said to her, "Come here, that you may eat of the bread and dip your piece of bread in the vinegar." So she sat beside the reapers; and he served her roasted grain, and she ate and was satisfied and had some left. (2:14)

The fifth attribute that we find in Boaz is that he is **considerate** of Ruth. He honors her in front of all the people. He gives her a place of esteem at the table. Boaz humbly serves her, doing what Jesus did when He girded himself about and washed His disciples' feet in John 13.

Pastor Chuck Smith tells this story from his own marriage: "I don't drink coffee, but Kay does. So in the morning I make the coffee and bring it to her." That has always stuck in my mind. Chuck doesn't drink coffee but, in consideration of Kay, he makes the coffee for her—and delivers it!

Good Housekeeping magazine had an article in it entitled "Romancing a Married Woman: Hints for a Clueless Husband." A passage that caught my attention read: "'One of the sweetest things my husband does is hang an umbrella on the door handle for me on a rainy day,' says Karen Wright, Assistant Director of

Marketing & Communications at Minnesota State University. 'It's a considerate and unexpected act that makes me fall even more in love with him, because it's just one more example of the way he considers my needs.'"[3] A woman finds it very attractive when a man is considerate.

Boaz Is Devoted

> When she rose to glean, Boaz commanded his servants, saying, "Let her glean even among the sheaves, and do not insult her. And also you shall purposely pull out for her some grain from the bundles and leave it that she may glean, and do not rebuke her." (2:15–16)

Boaz is unashamedly **devoted** and considerate of Ruth. He tells his servants, "Pull out the grain and leave it behind for her." He makes it known how he favors Ruth; he is not ashamed to show his devotion toward her.

Sometimes men have a "macho complex," in which they feel the need to give the appearance of being less emotional and unmoved. They don't want to show any sign of weakness or even any tenderness, lest people think less of them as a man. So they tend to be ashamed to publicly praise their wives, to be gentle and tenderhearted toward them, or to show how much they love them by displaying their affection for them. We should not be ashamed of our devotion for those we love. It is a very attractive trait to a woman when a man has unashamed devotion for her, like Boaz had toward Ruth.

Ruth Is Diligent

The next attribute in Ruth is found in chapter 2:17–23:

> So she gleaned in the field until evening. Then she beat out what she had gleaned, and it was about an ephah of barley. And she took it up and went into the city, and her

mother-in-law saw what she had gleaned. She also took it out and gave Naomi what she had left after she was satisfied. Her mother-in-law then said to her, "Where did you glean today and where did you work? May he who took notice of you be blessed." So she told her mother-in-law with whom she had worked and said, "The name of the man with whom I worked today is Boaz." And Naomi said to her daughter-in-law, "May he be blessed of the LORD who has not withdrawn his kindness to the living and to the dead!" Again Naomi said to her, "The man is our relative, he is one of our closest relatives." Then Ruth the Moabitess said, "Furthermore, he said to me, 'You shall stay close to my servants until they have finished all my harvest.'" And Naomi said to Ruth her daughter-in-law, "It is good, my daughter, that you go out with his maids, lest others fall upon you in another field." So she stayed close by the maids of Boaz in order to glean until the end of barley harvest and the wheat harvest. And she lived with her mother-in-law.

Ruth was **diligent**. The Bible says, "The soul of the diligent is made fat" (Proverbs 13:4). God rewards hard work. Proverbs 31 teaches us that diligence is one of the traits of a godly woman: "Strength and dignity are her clothing, and she smiles at the future. She opens her mouth in wisdom, and the teaching of kindness is on her tongue. She looks well to the ways of her household, and does not eat the bread of idleness" (vv. 25–27). That describes Ruth perfectly.

We will see this more clearly if we understand the times in which Ruth lived. There were fifty days from the wheat harvest to Pentecost. The barley harvest would have been two to three weeks before the wheat harvest. Ruth gleaned during both the barley harvest and in the wheat harvest—all those weeks. She was persistent; she followed through with the job, not giving up halfway into it. She never said, "This is too difficult, or this is boring; I quit."

Diligence is very attractive to a man. Often diligence is what advances a relationship through the hard times. Marriage needs partners who will persevere even when the going gets tough.

TEST YOURSELF

"What God proposes man disposes" is a saying that brings God's sovereignty and man's free will into focus. Choosing God's choice is just that: the providence of God brings people together, but then they must decide if that person really is God's choice for them to marry.

Being considerate, having unashamed devotion, and being diligent are three more traits that are attractive in a potential mate, and therefore helpful in our decision-making process.

1. Boaz' considerate acts and unashamed devotion demonstrate both private and public kindness.

   Which is more important, or more revealing, about a couple: how they treat one another in private or in public? Explain your answer.

2. Can speaking ill of your mate (or a friend) to others impact your feelings toward them? What do you think the consequences would be of continually speaking ill of someone you claim to care about—even in jest?

3. How does it make you feel when someone puts their mate down in front of you?

4. Diligence is a choice. It means "being persistent when times are tough; being thorough when the initial excitement or fun has worn off—seeing things through to completion."

  a. Do you tend to start things and not finish them?

  b. What impact could that have on a relationship?

5. Why is it attractive for a person to finish what they start?

NINE

Love and Marriage

We are going to put our study of the book of Ruth on pause for just a moment to ask the question: What makes marriage work? Then, in contrast, we will cover some reasons why people give up and bail out on their marital relationships.

One bright, beautiful Sunday morning, everyone in tiny Jonesville woke up early and went to their local church. Before service began, the townspeople sat in their pews, talking about their lives and families. Suddenly Satan appeared at the altar. Everyone started screaming and ran to the front door, trampling each other in their effort to get away from evil incarnate.

Soon everyone was gone but one man, who sat calmly in his pew, seemingly oblivious to the fact that he was in the presence of God's archenemy. That confused Satan a bit. He walked up to the man and said, "Hey, don't you know who I am?" The man answered, "Yep, I sure do." Satan asked, "Aren't you afraid of me?" and the man replied, "Nope, sure ain't." The devil, a little agitated by this time, said, "And why aren't you afraid of me?" To which the man calmly answered, "I've been married to your sister for 25 years."

That's a funny story, but I have counseled people who felt that they were married to one of the devil's relatives. Faced with this tragedy, I often wonder: "At what point did the relationship begin to fail? How did they get to the place where they have such disrespect and disdain for a person they once loved enough to marry?"

An Apologetic for Divorce

There was an article picked up recently by the *Honolulu Advertiser* by television producer Jennifer Just that had the byline "Maybe marriage, not divorce, is the problem." It struck me as an apologetic (or an attempt at justification) for her own divorce, after 15 years of marriage.

Ms. Just begins the article: "As I was filling out papers the other day—soon to join the 4 million in this year's divorce statistics—I wondered why I felt so ashamed, so on the verge of sending notes of apology to the 150 wedding guests my husband and I invited almost 15 years ago." She poses the question, "How can we live up to the impossibly high standards held for marriage nowadays?" "In the land of the free, married people are expected—at least according to such cultural bellwethers as women's magazines, TV and the federal government—to live, sleep and grow in tandem with the same person till death do them part, which statistically is 50 years and up if they marry at the normative age and die similarly. Married people are expected to feel passionately for the other person, but not too passionately, otherwise they risk 'losing their identity.'"

Then she says: "I suggest that to last a natural lifetime, marriages must be allowed to be more complex than this society accepts . . ." She points to former French president François Mitterrand, and the fact that his longtime mistress attended his funeral, as a possible explanation for France's divorce rate being half what it is in the US. She suggests we should reconsider the marriage vows and what the institution of marriage is about, allowing our unions to adjust for modern values; perhaps we need alternate types of relationships. Although she states, "I am not advocating that everyone have a mistress (or mister) on the side . . ." She pointed to the French as being a model, in that they have more open affairs.[4]

Ms. Just goes on to write that perhaps marriages should "be allowed to die a dignified death without stigmatizing the people who worked so hard to save it . . . With the shifts in lifestyles that people are prone to these days—very few people live in the same city or have the same job for 50 years—how can we expect a marriage to keep pace?"

She spoke of her 15-year marriage, how she and her husband raised their kids, got through the bad times, and were still friends. However, marriage changed for her. In the beginning two incomes were a great help, but now that she was in her mid-years, she didn't have need of a man's support, "not even to change a tire." She was quite self-sufficient; the one she began with was not the one with whom she wanted to retire.

So the problem, according to Jennifer Just, is not divorce but the American marriage. She points to these statistics: as of 1998, 19.4 million adults were divorced, affecting 20 million children—that's about 39 million people. She ends her article with the statement, "Some 39 million people can't all be wrong."

What a justification for her own divorce! It may be cathartic to write it down in the newspaper, but that doesn't make her conclusion accurate. Twenty million of those 39 million people she refers to are innocent children, *victims* of their parent's choice to divorce.

If she has been married 15 years and raised children during that time, then those kids are now teenagers. And when a husband and wife break up during their children's teen years, it is devastating for them. I had to live through that myself; it created scars in my life that took years to get over. A two-parent family is still the superior and ideal family.

Love Doesn't Make Marriage; Marriage Makes Love

When you make excuses for not being able to get along, and say the problem is the high standard for marriage, you are making an incorrect assessment of love and marriage. Love does not make a marriage; marriage makes and creates what love is supposed to be. You "learn" to love your mate in marriage.

Every marriage goes through difficult times; every marriage goes through trials and tribulations. However, marriage rescues love from immature feelings and the tyranny of emotions that on one day say, "I love you," and on the next say, "I don't love you." When you endure hard times, true love grows and a great marriage blossoms. Eventually, you will end up retiring with the mate you still passionately love.

Resolve is the key to staying on course. You resolve to fulfill your marriage vows "until death do us part." It is the way love grows and matures.

Danita and I have been married for over four decades, and we love each other more today than ever before. If left to our natural, fickle emotions and circumstances, however, we would have been another statistic in the divorce column years ago. Fortunately, Christ showed us that true love is His kind of *agape* love; it is self-sacrificing. We are more compatible now than ever before, even though at one time we were ready to throw in the towel like Jennifer Just. Presently we are living a marriage made in heaven and loving it. We have been tried and tested, but we didn't give up when we felt like bailing out. Now we are enjoying the fruit of what I believe every couple can have when Jesus is the center of the relationship. It begins and ends with the attributes we find infused in Boaz and Ruth.

The *Goel*

There is a beautiful theme to the book of Ruth. It centers around the tradition of the "kinsman redeemer," or *Goel* (in Hebrew), referred to 13 times throughout the book.

Keep in mind, the book of Ruth is not only a love story between Boaz and Ruth, but it is a love story between God and us. Ruth is a Moabitess, a Gentile; her husband Boaz is in the genealogy of King David, of whom Jesus Christ was born "according to the flesh" (Romans 1:3). Their story is one of redemption. Boaz, as the kinsman redeemer, is a type of Jesus Christ. He redeems Ruth—a Gentile who was without hope—marries her and has offspring by her.

Like Ruth, we Gentiles were separated from the promises of God, but by God's grace we are brought near by Christ's redemptive work on the cross. Ephesians 2:11–13 says, "Therefore remember, that formerly you, the Gentiles in the flesh . . . were at that time separate from Christ, excluded from the commonwealth of Israel, and strangers to the covenants of promise, having no hope and without God in the world. But now in Christ Jesus you who formerly were far off have been brought near by the blood of Christ." When Jesus died to redeem us, He made us heirs of His promises, and grafted us into the family of God (see Ephesians 3:6 and Romans 11:17). When Boaz married Ruth, he grafted her into the genealogy of Christ.

TEST YOURSELF

Resolve is the key to staying on course in a marriage. It takes commitment. All marriages will have ups and downs, times of great happiness, times of great sorrow, exciting times, and boring times. Throughout all of these variations, resolve to keep your marriage vows.

Remember, you have been brought near to God by the blood of Jesus Christ. There you will find the strength to endure the difficult times.

1. When times get tough, we tend to do one of two things: dig in and persevere or cut and run.

   Ecclesiastes 4:12 tells us that "a cord of three strands is not quickly torn apart."

   How does keeping Christ part of our marital relationship strengthen us when external forces want to pull us apart?

2. Today the ideal of commitment is eroding and being replaced by the ideal of romance. But commitment is the Bible's ideal. Commitment says:

> "I love you, and I plan to love you forever. I recognize that the romantic, excited feelings I have right now will fade. There will be times when we argue, times when we hurt each other, times when we simply can't see eye to eye; times when the frustrations of daily life are so great that we don't enjoy each other's company. I even recognize that in a lifetime of marriage, I will probably meet one or two other people I think are attractive too.
>
> "When those times come, I am committed to you, and I'll remember that. Even when my romantic feelings evaporate and I feel angry, lonely, or hurt, I will honor this commitment."

a. What does that resolve cost you?

b. What does that resolve gain for you?

Ruth Is Prepared

We return to the story in Ruth chapter 3. Ruth and Boaz are introduced to each other and sparks fly; there is definite chemistry. He is looking out for her, concerned for her wellbeing, and Ruth responds to him with appreciation and wonder. Notice what happens when Ruth comes home to her mother-in-law Naomi:

> And Naomi her mother-in-law said to her, "My daughter, shall I not seek security for you, that it may be well with you? And now is not Boaz our kinsman, with whose maids you were? Behold, he winnows barley at the threshing floor tonight." (3:1–2)

Naomi confides to Ruth, "This is one of our relatives. I know that he likes you and I know that you like him. He is going to be at the threshing floor tonight, winnowing (separating the wheat kernel from the husk)." She goes on:

> "Wash yourself therefore, and anoint yourself and put on your best clothes, and go down to the threshing floor; but do not make yourself known to the man until he has finished eating and drinking. And it shall be when he lies down, that you shall notice the place where he lies, and

you shall go and uncover his feet and lie down; then he will tell you what you should do." And she [Ruth] said to her, "All that you say I will do." (3:3–5)

Up until this point, Ruth's beauty has been "the hidden person of the heart." First Peter 3:3–4 says, "And let not your adornment be merely external—braiding the hair, and wearing gold jewelry, or putting on dresses; but let it be the hidden person of the heart, with the imperishable quality of a gentle and quiet spirit, which is precious in the sight of God." We have recognized Ruth's internal beauty, but now notice that Naomi encourages her to prepare herself for Boaz. Ruth is encouraged to beautify the outside.

We have all heard the expression "beauty is only skin deep." That certainly can be true. If her physical appearance is the only quality a woman spends time developing, she is likely to be a very shallow gal. But ugly is only skin deep too. If a woman thinks it is unimportant to look her best or unspiritual to develop and cultivate the outer countenance God has given her, she is selling herself short. So Naomi suggests something very practical to Ruth: spend some quality time on making yourself attractive to Boaz.

A while back my wife and some of the ladies at our church had a women's outreach in which they talked about fashion, how to dress, how to fix your hair and makeup, etc. She related this outward care to the inner beauty of the godly woman in Proverbs 31. They called the event Barn Painting, in reference to that old adage "If the barn needs painting, paint it." It was a humorous—and yet godly—way of saying, "Fix yourself up."

Naomi instructs Ruth on how to let Boaz know she is available. She advises her not to play mind games, not to play hard-to-get. She should be modest and innocent, not pushy or aggressive, but at the same time clearly available.

Sometimes there are very attractive single people who love the Lord, who have the inward qualities and the outward looks, but they just don't make themselves available. They hide out, almost as though they expect God to drop a mate down from heaven and leave them at their doorstep. Naomi wisely counsels Ruth to make herself available to a quality man like Boaz.

Ruth Is Submitted

> So she [Ruth] went down to the threshing floor and did according to all that her mother-in-law had commanded her. When Boaz had eaten and drunk and his heart was merry, he went to lie down at the end of the heap of grain; and she came secretly and uncovered his feet and lay down. And it happened in the middle of the night that the man was startled and bent forward; and behold, a woman was lying at his feet. (3:6–8)

This passage references an unusual custom in the Jewish culture that we need to explain.

If you were Boaz, it would be quite startling to wake up in the middle of the night to find a woman lying at your feet! Understand, there is no sexual connotation here; this is not a lurid scene or anything provocative. In our scandal-ridden society people might want to read something torrid into this scene, but don't, because it is actually an innocent and beautiful setting. In fact, this was a perfectly proper courting ritual in the Jewish culture of the time.

> And he said, "Who are you?" And she answered, "I am Ruth your maid. So spread your covering over your maid, for you are a close relative." (3:9)

Jewish law said that if a man died, his next of kin was to raise up offspring for him from his widow. This law was intended to perpetuate the family name so it would not die out in Israel. We read in Deuteronomy 25:5–6: "When brothers live together and one of them dies and has no son, the wife of the deceased shall not be married outside the family to a strange man. Her husband's brother shall go in to her and take her to himself as wife and perform the duty of a husband's brother to her. And it shall be that the firstborn whom she bears shall assume the name of his dead brother, that his name may not be blotted out from Israel."

Ruth, at the instruction of Naomi, was signaling to Boaz that she was available, saying "Cover me, if you will, for you are a close relative. I am available for you to redeem, for you to marry, if you are willing to cover me."

This willingness to be covered, to be **submitted** is an attractive trait in a woman. It means she is willing to come under the leadership or authority of a husband. Genesis 3:16 says in part, "Your desire shall be for your husband, and he will rule over you." First Corinthians 11:3 says, "Christ is the head of every man, and the man is the head of a woman, and God is the head of Christ."

What Emasculates a Man

It is very attractive and very humbling for a man like Boaz to know that his wife is willing to be led by him. It is very attractive for a single man to know that the woman he is interested in is willing to be covered by his headship and led by his leadership.

By the same token, it is very emasculating for a man to feel that he has to fight with his wife for the right to be head of the home. Wrestling with her to function in his God-given role weakens the man. So it is very attractive when a woman is willing to be covered, when she says, "I want you to be the head, the leader, and the protector of our home."

Proverbs 14:1 makes a keen observation: "The wise woman builds her house, but the foolish tears it down with her own hands." Sadly, this tearing down can be the result of a wife refusing to let her husband assume his role as head of the home.

TEST YOURSELF

In this section we've talked about two subjects that can be controversial, both in the church and in the world: inner beauty versus outer beauty, and submission.

1. God's guidelines regarding clothing and dress are very general. Christian women are to dress "with proper clothing, modestly and discreetly" (I Timothy 2:9). In other words, a Christian woman should not be attracting undue attention to herself by wearing clothes that are provocative, suggestive, or outrageous.

   That does not mean, however, that Christian women should be drab, colorless, or tasteless dressers, so out of step with the fashions of society that they stand out like the proverbial sore thumb. Clothes can be fashionable without being immodest or peculiar.

   a. For everyone:

   Where is the balance between inner and outer beauty?

   b. For women:

   Which do you work on more easily: inner or outer beauty? What can you change to achieve a better balance?

c. For men:

Which appeals to you more: inner or outer beauty? What do you think motivates that choice?

2. Prior to making herself available to Boaz, Ruth first made herself available to Naomi. She sought Naomi's wellbeing, serving her wholeheartedly. In the midst of this care, Naomi gave her instruction that would impact Ruth's own life for the best.

   Matthew 6 records Jesus' encouragement for us to entrust our earthly needs to the loving care of our heavenly Father. He tells us, "Seek first His kingdom and His righteousness; and all these things shall be added to you" (vs. 33).

   a. Are you available to the Lord, to serve Him with the same attitude of selfless devotion with which Ruth served Naomi?

   b. Are you involved in activities that will bring you into contact with like-minded people, for example: home fellowships, church potlucks, group outings (sports events, theater, recreational activities, etc.)?

c. Are you able to trust that as you serve the Lord and put yourself into places and situations that honor Him and make you available to meet others, that God will meet your needs?

d. If you are struggling with that trust, can you think of anything you can begin doing to strengthen your faith in this area?

3. Submission is a controversial subject in the church today. Those who do not understand the idea of *covering* or what the Bible means by a woman *submitting* to her husband, think in terms of coercion or oppression. But biblical submission is not forced obedience; it is an act of *yielded surrender*. It is done of one's own accord, from a position of strength, not weakness. A women entrusts herself to the Lord and to her husband, not because she is forced, but because she *chooses* to do so.

a. What are the challenges for a wife, with respect to submission?

b. What are the challenges for a husband, with respect to submission?

c. How does a wife's submission show support for her husband?

d. When a wife submits to her husband, who is the real recipient of the act: her, her husband, or the Lord?

Explain your answer.

ELEVEN

Boaz Praises Ruth

> Then he said, "May you be blessed of the LORD, my
> daughter. You have shown your last kindness to be better
> than the first by not going after young men, whether poor
> or rich." (3:10)

What was Ruth's first kindness? Her selfless devotion to her mother-in-law! She was looking out for Naomi. Boaz tells her that this last kindness is even greater. He is telling her, "Ruth, with your looks, personality, and the way you hold yourself, you could have had any man you wanted, rich or poor, young or old. You could have used your feminine mystique to get what you wanted. But you didn't. You chose to wait on the Lord for His timing and providence." Boaz praises her for such a highly prized character quality.

> "Now, my daughter, do not fear. I will do for you whatever
> you ask, for all my people in the city know that you are a
> woman of excellence. Now it is true I am a close relative;
> however, there is a relative closer than I. Remain this night,
> and when morning comes, if he will redeem you, good; let
> him redeem you. But if he does not wish to redeem you,
> then I will redeem you, as the LORD lives. Lie down until
> morning." (3:11–13)

It is very important for a woman to be **praised** by the man she loves. It should begin during courtship, and then the praises should continue throughout the marriage. It affirms and cultivates a woman's sense of self-worth and self-respect.

Some people downplay this idea of a woman's self-image being nurtured and supported, but I have seen women who lived with men who were brutes. Women who are married to such men reflect on their faces how they are treated. A once young, vibrant, and beautiful woman now looks haggard and older than her years. Before she got married she was radiant and glowing, but after ten years of marriage she is worn down and drawn out, with no incentive to make herself attractive.

When a man praises a woman it affects her inwardly and that shows outwardly. God created her to be praised by her husband. When God brought Eve to Adam, his first words were "This is it!" (Genesis 2:23 TLB). It was an exclamation of praise! Women have desired praise ever since. Praise tells her she is has worth, that she is valuable to her man. It does for her what Boaz did for Ruth when he said to her, "You are a woman of excellence" (Ruth 3:11).

Boaz brags about Ruth behind her back and then highly esteems her face-to-face. A man must never, ever tear down his mate, but always build her up; it is very attractive to a woman when a man praises her.

Boaz Is Protective

So she lay at his feet until morning, and she rose before one could recognize another; and then he said, "Let it not be known that the woman came to the threshing floor." Again he said, "Give me the cloak that is on you and hold it." So she held it, and he measured six measures of barley and laid it on her. Then she went into the city. And when she came to her mother-in-law, she said, "How did it go, my daughter?" And she told her all that the man had done for her. And she said, "These six measures of barley he gave me, for he said, 'Do not go to your mother-in-law empty-handed.'" Then she said, "Wait, my daughter, until you know how the matter turns out; for the man will not rest until he has settled it today." (3:14–18)

The eighth thing Boaz did, which is very attractive to a woman, is he **protected** Ruth's reputation. He instructs her to rise before anyone can recognize her and not to tell anyone that she was there at the threshing floor.

A man should protect the woman he loves. He should not expose her weaknesses. He should not leave her vulnerable to the speculation of others, or put her in a place where people might think of her in a disrespectful way.

I once counseled an unmarried couple where the man had allowed the woman to be put in a compromising situation, exposing her to the temptations of the enemy and the speculations of others. Maybe his car was parked at her apartment until all hours of the night. Or perhaps there was excessive physical contact between them. That gave Satan an opportunity, because the man was not guarding her against temptation. The result was people questioned the genuineness of her faith.

If a man disregards a woman's reputation when courting, not caring what others might think or say about her, she should drop him like a hot potato. It will only get worse after marriage. Godly women should not allow themselves to get into such compromising situations.

I have a vivid memory of a fellow in the church who outwardly appeared to be very spiritual. He met and later became engaged to a woman in the fellowship. After a few months she came to me crying, saying that he was putting her into compromising situations, taking the relationship to a physical level with which she was not comfortable.

She said, "Since I became a Christian, I've always wanted to marry a godly man who would lead me in the things of the Lord. I thought I found that man, but now I'm not sure."

In my office with both of them present, I looked at him and, although he was a well-established brother in the church, serving, going on mission trips, always talking about Jesus, I told her, "Drop him like a rock! Apparently he is not the spiritual man that he made himself out to be."

Unfortunately, she didn't; and she went through a few miserable years of marriage until she could stand it no longer, and the relationship dissolved. If a man does not respect a woman and does not protect her during their courtship and engagement period, it is unlikely that he will protect her after they get married.

Boaz Is Thoughtful

This passage in chapter 3 also shows that Boaz was **thoughtful** toward Ruth's family. He was sensitive to the fact that they recently returned with nothing, and that there was no one to help them. Naomi was too frail to go out into the field herself to glean, and Boaz sensed she was coaching Ruth about what just took place at the threshing floor. So he lavished Ruth with grain and told her, "Bring this to your mother-in-law." He was probably thinking, "Way to go, Naomi!" and his gratitude was reflected in his gift.

Good Housekeeping magazine recently had an article entitled "How to Romance a Married Woman: Ideas for a Clueless Husband." One section of the article, subtitled "Deflected Wooing," read, "Just this past week, it was my mother's birthday and my husband bought her a beautiful bouquet of flowers," says Liza O'Neill, an account executive for a public relations firm in Florida. "To be honest, I felt when he did that, it was a way of wooing me."[5]

Boaz had a good insight and he perfected it long before *Good Housekeeping* thought to write about it. When Boaz sent such a generous gift to Naomi, it translated to Ruth that he deeply cared for *her* welfare as well.

Boaz Is Enthusiastic

Naomi picks up on the next characteristic of Boaz that is attractive to a woman. She tells Ruth in 3:18 that *"the man will not rest until he has settled it today."* It is attractive to a woman when other people see that a man is **enthusiastic** for the one he loves. Naomi saw and commented on Boaz's interest in Ruth. It has great value for a woman when a man has infectious enthusiasm for their relationship.

Recently my wife Danita and I were in Colorado teaching at a marriage retreat. We had arrived in Colorado Springs a day early and took some time to check out the small town. At lunchtime we were driving around looking for a place to eat. Deciding on a spot, we got out of the car, holding hands as we walked into the restaurant. We sat down, got our menus, ordered, and then prayed for our meal. We were seated in an outside dining area with only a few other people around. We ate our lunch and after about 45 minutes or so, we prepared to leave.

A few tables away from us, two girls were having their lunch. As we got up to leave they asked, "Are you two Christians?" We said, "Yes, we are," and we struck up a conversation with them. They told us, "When we saw you come in, you were holding hands. We thought something was up with you. Then we saw you praying and we knew there was something different about you." For the next half-hour, we talked and had great fellowship in the Lord.

My point? People are watching you. People notice how you interact as a couple, how you treat each other. They watch as the guy walks two feet ahead of the girl. They notice if you always come in separate cars. They are looking to see if you are a couple and what kind of relationship you have. If there isn't any enthusiasm in your relationship, they see that too.

Naomi notices and comments on the enthusiasm Boaz has for Ruth. This trait is very attractive to a woman, as well as noticed by those watching you.

Pastor Chuck Smith, of Calvary Chapel Costa Mesa, California, was in Hawaii a couple years back, giving me some pointers regarding the construction of our new church campus. As I was taking him and one of the builders back to their hotel, we got stuck in afternoon traffic. (Isn't that the dream of every pastor: getting stuck in traffic with Chuck, affording the time to ask him every question we've ever had about the ministry?)

As we sat in the car, I was able to attend a ten-minute marriage conference put on by Chuck himself. There were terrible wildfires burning in California at the time, putting Calvary Chapel's conference center at risk. He had called his wife Kay to find out how things were going.

Overhearing the joy, tenderness, and enthusiasm in his voice when Kay answered the phone was a seminar all in itself. As they spoke, I learned and was convicted and encouraged all at the same time. That is just one reason why we love Chuck and Kay Smith so much. Their lives truly are an epistle of Christ "written not with ink, but with the Spirit of the living God" (II Corinthians 3:3).

People are watching and listening to you, and they are determining whether or not there is any real enthusiasm in your relationship.

TEST YOURSELF

Boaz praised Ruth, protected her virtue, and was enthusiastic about her, all which demonstrated how much he *valued* Ruth. He valued her because he loved her, and he showed that love with deeds of kindness and subtle words of admiration.

1. How do you represent the people you love to others?

    a. Do you discuss their faults? Do you praise them?

    b. How can you tell the difference between praising your loved one for *his or her* glory and praising them for *your* glory?

2. First Thessalonians 5:22 tells us to "abstain from all **appearance** of evil."

    How would you apply that principle to dating/courtship?

3. Along with a woman's virtue and reputation, what other things should a man protect?

4. Thoughtful people don't wait, they create opportunities to bless others. It is a conscious act, a habit that can be developed.

   a. How can thoughtfulness help a relationship grow?

   b. How can carelessness destroy a relationship?

5. In looking at your most significant relationship, can you think of something that demonstrates any enthusiasm?

TWELVE

Boaz Pays the Price to Redeem Ruth

The scene changes and the whole redemption process is laid out before us as Boaz goes through the legal rite of acquiring Ruth. We begin in chapter 4:

> Now Boaz went up to the gate and sat down there; and behold, the close relative of whom Boaz had spoke was passing by, so he said, "Turn aside, friend, sit down here." So he turned aside and sat down. And he took ten men of the elders of the city and said, "Sit down here." So they sat down. Then he said to the closest relative, "Naomi, who has come back from the land of Moab, has to sell the piece of land which belonged to our brother Elimelech. So I thought to inform you, saying, 'Buy it before those who are sitting here, and before the elders of my people. If you will redeem it, redeem it; but if not, tell me that I may know; for there is no one but you to redeem it, and I am after you.'" And he said, "I will redeem it." (4:1–4)

Back in ancient times people went to the city gate to socialize, conduct business, make deals and verify agreements. It was where legal transactions took place. The city gate was not like the gates we use today, made of wood or metal and used to keep people out and secure our privacy. Ancient gates had rooms attached to them, nooks and niches in which the elders could sit and talk over the affairs of the day.

This is where Boaz went to find his next of kin, along with ten of the city's leaders. He made the proposal to his relative in front of all of those leaders, saying, "You have the right to redeem the field of our close relative Elimelech. Do you want to redeem it?" The man answered, "Sure! I'm not one to pass up a deal on an extra piece of property. I would love to redeem it."

At this point all the requirements needed to make the deal official were in play: they were at the city gate with ten elders present. It was then that Boaz dropped a bombshell. It was his ace in the hole and he knew it:

> Then Boaz said, "On the day you buy the field from the hand of Naomi, you must also acquire Ruth the Moabitess, the widow of the deceased, in order to raise up the name of the deceased on his inheritance." (4:5)

What was his ace in the hole? If the relative wanted to buy Elimelech's field he must also marry Mahlon's widow, Elimelech's daughter-in-law, and raise up a son to him so that his family name would not perish from the earth. In other words, Ruth came with the deal!

Boaz already anticipated the man's answer:

> And the closest relative said, "I cannot redeem it for myself, lest I jeopardize my own inheritance. Redeem it for yourself; you may have my right of redemption, for I cannot redeem it." Now this was the custom in former times in Israel concerning the redemption and the exchange of land to confirm any matter: a man removed his sandal and gave

it to another; and this was the manner of attestation in Israel. So the closest relative said to Boaz, "Buy it for yourself." And he removed his sandal. (4:6–8)

This was a fascinating custom, based on the Mosaic law recorded in Deuteronomy 25:7–10: "But if the man does not desire to take his brother's wife, then his brother's wife shall go up to the gate to the elders and say, 'My husband's brother refuses to establish a name for his brother in Israel; he is not willing to perform the duty of a husband's brother to me.' Then the elders of his city shall summon him and speak to him. And if he persists and says, 'I do not desire to take her,' then his brother's wife shall come to him in the sight of the elders, and pull his sandal off his foot and spit in his face; and she shall declare, 'Thus it is done to the man who does not build up his brother's house.' In Israel his name shall be called, 'The house of him whose sandal is removed.'"

So the man would leave the gate of the city without a sandal. As he hobbled home with one bare foot, all the citizens of the city would identify him as "the man who would not build up his brother's house." Even so, his wife was probably happy and relieved.

In some cases, it just would not have been practical to "build up your brother's house." It was a known fact that Boaz was next in line; Naomi and Ruth would not be abandoned. So it was not cruel or uncaring for this relative to refuse the right of redemption; it was prudent and logical. So rather than spitting in the man's face when he removed his sandal, Boaz gratefully redeemed the land and Ruth.

Boaz Has Unselfish Love

Then Boaz said to the elders and all the people, "You are witnesses today that I have bought from the hand of Naomi all that belonged to Elimelech and all that belonged to Chilion and Mahlon. Moreover, I have acquired Ruth the Moabitess, the widow of Mahlon, to be my wife in order to raise up the name of the deceased on his inheritance, so that the name of the deceased may not be cut off from his brothers or from the court of his birth place; you are witnesses today." And all the people who were in the court, and the elders, said, "We are witnesses. May the LORD make the woman who is coming into your home like Rachel and Leah, both of whom built the house of Israel; and may you achieve wealth in Ephrathah and become famous in Bethlehem. Moreover, may your house be like the house of Perez whom Tamar bore to Judah, through the offspring which the LORD shall give you by this young woman." (4:9–12)

So we come to the final attribute of Boaz for men to emulate: **unselfish love**. He goes out of his way for the woman he loves, plotting, planning, and going the second mile. Boaz rearranges his busy schedule to gain Ruth's affection. It sends the message that he is willing to do for her above and beyond the call of duty. His actions demonstrate that he places a high value—top priority—on this relationship. He is unselfishly in love with Ruth.

One whole chapter of the book of Ruth is devoted to this act of redemption. Everything else is leading up to this important event.

This attribute of unselfish love was the primary motivation for Jesus in His ministry. The Bible says in Matthew 13:44: "The kingdom of heaven is like a treasure hidden in the field, which a man found and hid; and from joy over it he goes and sells all that he has, and buys that field." Notice that the man sold all that he had to buy the field in order to gain the treasure. It is a parable [an earthly story of a heavenly truth] illustrating the extent to which God has gone to redeem mankind.

The *man* in the parable "goes and sells all," meaning that God gave the most precious gift He had, His Son Jesus, to redeem the field. "For God so loved the world, that He gave His only begotten

Son, that whoever believes in Him should not perish, but have eternal life" (John 3:16). While the field is the world, it is the treasure *in* the world that God is interested in obtaining.

You and I are that treasure! The love of God draws us to Himself and to repentance. And in the same way, it is very attractive for a man to have unselfish love for the woman he is courting.

TEST YOURSELF

In order for Boaz to purchase Elimelech's field, he had to marry Ruth. That brings up an interesting point: When you commit to a person, you get a family along with them.

1. How involved in your life is your family?

   How involved in his/her family is your potential mate?

   a. How would it impact your relationship with a potential mate if they did not get along with your family?

   b. How would it impact your relationship with a potential mate if they did not get along with *their own* family?

2. Boaz also demonstrated unselfish love for Ruth. That is the kind of love Christ has for us: unselfish, unconditional, *agape* love. Ephesians 5:25 tells us: "Husbands, love your wives, just as Christ also loved the church and gave Himself up for her . . ."

Read I Corinthians 13:4–8a, and write down what you learn about God's love:

a. Love is _____,

    love is _____,

    and is not _____.

b. Love does not _____

    and is not _____.

c. Love does not _____,

    it does not _____,

    is not _____,

    does not _____.

d. Love does not _____,

    but does _____.

e. Love _____ all things,

    _____ all things,

    _____ all things,

    and _____ all things.

f. Love never _____.

Which of those characteristics of Boaz' and Jesus' love challenge you the most as a mate or potential mate? What **specifically** will you do to strengthen this area?

The Rest of the Story

Happily Ever After

How does the book of Ruth conclude? It is a happily-ever-after ending. Boaz redeems Ruth, marries her, and they are blessed with offspring, even as the elders and townspeople had prayed for them.

> So Boaz took Ruth, and she became his wife, and when he went in to her And the LORD enabled her to conceive, and she gave birth to a son. Then the women said to Naomi, "Blessed be the LORD who has not left you without a redeemer today, and may his name become famous in Israel. May he also be to you a restorer of life and a sustainer of your old age; for your daughter-in-law, who loves you and is better to you than seven sons, has given birth to him." Then Naomi took the child and laid him in her lap, and became his nurse. And the neighbor women gave him a name, saying, "A son has been born to Naomi." So they named him Obed. He is the father of Jesse, the father of David.
>
> Now these are the generations of Perez: to Perez was born Hezron, and to Hezron was born Ram, and to Ram, Amminadab, and to Amminadab was born Nahshon, and to Nahshon, Salmon, and to Salmon was born Boaz, and to Boaz, Obed, and to Obed was born Jesse, and to Jesse, David. (4:13–22)

When we see how things turned out for Naomi, who had begrudged her own circumstances not long before, we marvel at the faithfulness of God. From heaven's point of view, God had destined her to be a *blessed* woman; but from her point of view, she lamented, "Do not call me **pleasant** [Naomi]; call me **bitter** [Mara], for the Almighty has dealt **very bitterly** with me" (1:20). Naomi did not see the great blessing God had in store for her.

It is easy to get to a place of discouragement when we cannot see the complete plan of God for our lives. Doubt obscures the good God has for us, leaving us sulking and miserable. Trusting in the Lord always pays big dividends, however. The Bible tells us in Isaiah 26:3 that God will keep us in perfect peace because we trust in Him.

The genealogy given in Ruth 4:18–22 tells us that Ruth is King David's great-grandmother, and Naomi his great-great-grandmother. But more than that, it also places them in the lineage of the Messiah (Matthew 1:1–5). It was the hope and dream of every woman and mother in Israel to give birth to the Messiah. How truly blessed of God were these two women!

When we fall on hard times like Naomi, we can begin to feel as though God is against us. If we could see through eyes of faith, however, we would discover the truth about our gracious heavenly Father: "For I know the plans that I have for you," declares the LORD, "plans for welfare and not for calamity to give you a future and a hope" (Jeremiah 29:11). We cannot see what the future holds for us, but God can. We need to trust Him. He knows that just a little ways further, right around the next bend, just a few more steps and we will see His glorious plan unfold before our very eyes, as Naomi did. For now, we need faith.

Conclusion

How do we respond to this incredible love story? Is it just a dream come true for Ruth and Boaz, or can this kind of scenario happen to couples today? Can it happen in your life?

I am convinced that the Lord is "the same yesterday and today, yes and forever" (Hebrews 13:8).

Sometimes a person might feel they will never find true love, or that the perfect mate—the one who will complete them—will never come along. Actually, in one sense that is true: if you are *on the hunt* to find Mr. or Mrs. Right, you likely will end up very disappointed.

A woman in our fellowship came up to me one day, after having been AWOL from church for some time. She had been *on the hunt* for a husband, going to classes, retreats, singles fellowships, and so on, and nothing happened for her. Now she was mad at God for all the effort she put into looking, and for all the time and money she spent on preparing herself for marriage. In the middle of her tirade about how God had let her down, all I could think was, "I pity the poor fellow she *does* manage to get her claws into!"

First things first. Neither Ruth nor Boaz was *on the hunt* for a mate. They waited on God to prepare their individual hearts and build godly character within them. They did their part by allowing God to work within them, and then God did His part through His providence to bring the two of them together. They were *naturally* brought together by circumstances in a *supernatural* way.

There is no concrete formula for this kind of thing. God's ways are not our ways, and His ways are beyond finding out. We can know for certain, however, that for those who "seek first the kingdom of God"—as a personal priority—He will add "all these things" unto them . . . even you!

May God richly bless you.

REVIEW TEST

Let's see how well you remember what traits we have seen in Boaz and Ruth that make them a man and woman worth marrying. Using only your Bible, read through these portions of the book of Ruth and summarize the attributes you find in this amazing man and woman.

Eight Attributes Seen in Ruth:

1. She is _____ (1:14–18)

2. She is _____ (1:22–2:2)

3. She is _____ (2:10)

4. She is _____ (2:13)

5. She is _____ (2:13)

6. She is _____ (2:17–23)

7. She is _____ (3:1–5)

8. She is _____ (3:6–8)

Eleven Attributes Seen in Boaz:

1. He is _____ (2:3–4)

2. He is _____ (2:5–7)

3. He is _____ (2:8–9)

4. He is _____ (2:11–12)

5. He is _____ (2:14)

6. He is _____ (2:15–16)

7. He _____ (3:10–11)

8. He is _____ (3:14–18)

9. He is _____ (3:14–18)

10. He is _____ (3:14–18)

11. He has _____ (4:9–12)

A Closing Prayer

Ruth is a beautiful book of redemption, but it is also a biblical look at what is attractive in a mate. And so I leave you with this final word of prayer:

- *For those of you who will remain single throughout your lives:*

I pray that you would embrace the godly attitudes and characteristics found in Boaz and Ruth for the glory of God and the furtherance of His kingdom.

- *For those of you who are single now but will one day be married:*

I pray that you would allow the Holy Spirit to lead you to a mate with these qualities and that you would desire to be this type of husband or wife.

- *For those of you who are already married:*

I pray that you would continue to develop these characteristics in yourself and appreciate them in your mate, in order to keep your marriage on track, growing and maturing into the best relationship it can possibly be.

A SPECIAL MESSAGE

Our Kinsman Redeemer

Boaz is a type of heaven's kinsman redeemer, Jesus Christ. There were certain obligations that the *Goel* (Hebrew for "redeemer") had to fulfill in order to redeem someone or something. First, he had to be a *blood* relative. Second, he had to be *able* to pay the price of redemption. Third, he had to be *willing* to redeem. Fourth, he had to be *free* to redeem. Boaz met every obligation necessary to redeem Ruth, and Jesus Christ has fulfilled all the requirements necessary to redeem us.

Jesus is a *blood* relative

- "God was in Christ reconciling the world to Himself . . ." (II Corinthians 5:19).

- "And the Word [Jesus] became flesh, and dwelt among us, and we beheld His glory, glory as of the only begotten from the Father, full of grace and truth" (John 1:14).

- "Since then the children share in flesh and blood, He Himself likewise also partook of the same, that through death He might render powerless him who had the power of death, that is, the devil" (Hebrews 2:14).

- "But when the fullness of the time came, God sent forth His Son, born of a woman, born under the Law, in order that He might redeem those who were under the Law, that we might receive the adoption as sons" (Galatians 4:4–5).

- "So also it is written, 'The first MAN, Adam, BECAME A LIVING SOUL.' The last Adam became a life-giving spirit" (I Corinthians 15:45).

All of us are born of the first Adam, and therefore born in sin. Jesus, the last Adam, is without sin, and is our *blood* relative by the fact that He took upon Himself flesh and blood.

He is *able* to pay the price:

- "Knowing that you were not redeemed with perishable things like silver or gold from your futile way of life inherited from your forefathers, but with precious blood, as of a lamb unblemished and spotless, the blood of Christ" (I Peter 1:18–19).

- "And when you were dead in your transgressions and the uncircumcision of your flesh, He made you alive together with Him, having forgiven us all our transgressions, having canceled out the certificate of debt consisting of decrees against us and which was hostile to us; and He has taken it out of the way, having nailed it to the cross. When He had disarmed the rulers and authorities, He made a public display of them, having triumphed over them through Him" (Colossians 2:13–15).

He is *willing* to pay the price:

- "Fixing our eyes on Jesus, the author and perfecter [finisher] of faith, who for the joy set before Him endured the cross, despising the shame, and has sat down at the right hand of the throne of God" (Hebrews 12:2).

- "For I have come down from heaven, not to do My own will, but the will of Him who sent Me" (John 6:38).

- "Now My soul has become troubled; and what shall I say, 'Father, save Me from this hour'? But for this purpose I came to this hour" (John 12:27).

He is *free* to redeem:

- "The next day he saw Jesus coming to him, and said, "Behold, the Lamb of God who takes away the sin of the world!" (John 1:29).

- "No one has taken it [my life] away from Me, but I lay it down on My own initiative. I have authority to lay it down, and I have authority to take it up again. This commandment I received from My Father" (John 10:18).

- "How much more will the blood of Christ, who through the eternal Spirit offered Himself without blemish to God, cleanse your conscience from dead works to serve the living God?" (Hebrews 9:14).

FOR FURTHER READING

Elliot, Elisabeth. *Love Has a Price Tag*. Regal Books.

Getz, Gene. *The Measure of a Man*. Regal Books.

Karssen, Gien. *Her Name is Woman*. Navpress Publishing Group.

Redpath, Alan. *The Making of a Man of God: Lessons from the Life of David*. Revell.

Shedd, Charlie. *Letters to Philip*. Doubleday.

Stonebraker, Bill. *Spiritual Warfare in Marriage*. Calvary Chapel.

Wheat, Dr. Ed. *Love Life for Every Married Couple: How to Fall in Love, Stay in Love, Rekindle Your Love*. Zondervan.

And also:

Edwards, Gene. *A Tale of Three Kings: A Study in Brokenness*. Tyndale House Publishers. *(A great book on God's providence—not taking matters into your own hands.)*

ABOUT THE AUTHOR

Bill Stonebraker came to Hawaii from California with his wife Danita and their oldest daughter in 1967. They now have three children and twelve grandchildren. Bill established himself in a surfboard-making business, and while still living in Sunset Beach on Oahu's North Shore, made a life-changing commitment to Jesus Christ.

A Bible study that began in the Stonebraker's home in the 70s grew into the North Shore Christian Fellowship, affiliated with Calvary Chapel ministries, from which Bill received his ordination. In 1982, Bill turned NSCF over to his associate pastor and began Calvary Chapel of Honolulu, where he currently pastors.

The church moved into the downtown Honolulu area in 1987. The impact made by the congregation in that urban neighborhood earned the church special recognition from the mayor of Honolulu.

A new church-school campus was designed and constructed in Aiea, a more central location on the island, and was dedicated in May of 2004. It houses the church, KLHT Radio Station (1040AM), The Chapel Bookstore & Calvary Café, a Calvary Chapel Bible College extension campus, a preschool, and a Christian school with enrollment covering kindergarten through 7th Grade (expanding to 8th grade).

The church is involved in missionary endeavors around the world, most recently in Cherokee, Iowa; Japan, Tahiti, and Vanuatu. Short- and long-term mission work has also been done in the Philippines, China, Fiji, Hungary, the Marshall Islands, Mexico, Nepal, Poland, Russia, Thailand, Uganda, and Ethiopia.

ENDNOTES

[1] The Barna Group has granted non-exclusive permission for the English language to use the article in Barna Update, August 6, 2001. www.barna.org

[2] Peterson, Karen S. June 4, 2003. "Study Suggests Teen Sex Linked to Depression, Suicide Tries." *USA TODAY*.

[3] Kaufman, Joanne. February 2003. "Romancing a Married Woman: Hints for Clueless Husbands." *Good Housekeeping*, pg. 78.

[4] Just, Jennifer. June 2003. "Maybe Marriage is Problem." *Honolulu Advertiser*.

[5] Kaufman.